# THE COMPLETE
## TINY BOOK OF

C000298049

HarperCollins*Publishers*

HarperCollins*Publishers*
77–85 Fulham Palace Road, Hammersmith,
London W6 8JB

www.**fire**and**water**.com

This edition 2000
9 8 7 6 5 4 3 2 1

First published by Angus & Robertson
Previously published by Fontana 1992
Reprinted twice

A catalogue record for this book is
available from the British Library

ISBN 0-00-711320-X

Printed and bound in Hong Kong by
Printing Express Ltd

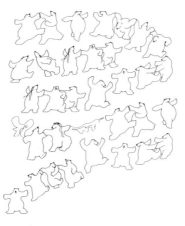

... because we are all holding
each other through a dance of
joy and love.

I embrace with honour
my daughter, Ann Maureen Keating,
and all those at her special place
of learning for the developmentally
disabled, St Vincent School in
Santa Barbara, California.
I embrace with honour my son,
Matthew Roy Keating,
my father and mother,
Roy and Minnie Armistead, and my
sister Christine Ann Armistead.
I embrace with gratitude
Golda Clendenin and Helen Colton
who inspired me.
My friends and colleagues at

Woodview-Calabasas Hospital,
and my friends
Lynne and Maureen De Boer,
Margie Rinehart,
Wendy McCarty Wong,
Anita Liggett, Francie White,
Cathy Davis, Judith Harkins,
Sue Von Baeyer and
Christina Essmana for
supporting me.
I embrace those at Esalen Institute
for teaching me, David Gorton
for believing in me and
Fred Schloessinger,
for holding me with love.

hug (hug) v.t. hugged, hugging, hugs.
1. to clasp or hold closely,
especially in one's arms; embrace
or enfold, as in affection
2. to cherish, hold fast
3. to keep very close to
hug n. An affectionate embrace
(from Scandinavian, akin to old
Norse hugga, to comfort, console)
hug therapy n.
1. The practice of administering
hugs for the purpose of curing or
healing, or of preserving health
2. Treatment of disease through the
simple, physical means of hugging

# About hugging and huggers

# Theory

Touch is not only nice. It's needed. Scientific research supports the theory that stimulation by touch is absolutely necessary for our physical as well as our emotional well-being.

Therapeutic touch, recognised as an essential tool for healing, is now part of nurses' training in several large

A hug makes you feel good
all day.

medical centres. Touch is used to help relieve pain and depression and anxiety, to bolster patients' will to live, to help premature babies — who have been deprived of touch in their incubators — grow and thrive.

Various experiments have shown that touch can:

Make us feel better about ourselves and our surroundings;

Have a positive effect on children's language development and IQ;

Cause measurable physiological changes in the toucher and the touched.

We are just beginning to understand the power of touch.

While there are many forms of touching, we propose that hugging is a very special one that contributes in a major way to healing and health.

# Rationale

HUGGING

Feels good

Dispels loneliness

Overcomes fears

Opens doors to feelings

Builds self-esteem ('Wow! *She*
actually wants to hug *me*!')

Fosters altruism ('I can't
believe it, but I actually *want*
to hug that old son-of-a-gun!')

Slows down ageing; huggers
stay younger longer

Helps curb appetite; we eat
less when we are nourished by
hugs — and when our arms are
busy wrapped around others

# HUGGING ALSO

Eases tension

Fights insomnia

Keeps arm and shoulder
muscles in condition

Provides stretching exercise if
you are short

Provides stooping exercise if
you are tall

Offers a wholesome alternative
to promiscuity

Offers a healthy, safe alternative to alcohol and other drug abuse (*better hugs than drugs!*)

Affirms physical being

Is democratic; anyone is eligible for a hug

Is ecologically sound, does not upset the environment

Is energy-efficient, saves heat

Is portable

Requires no special equipment

Demands no special setting;
any place from a doorstep to
an executive conference room,
from a church parlour to a
football field, is a fine place
for a hug!

Makes happy days happier

Makes impossible days
possible

Imparts feelings of belonging

Fills up empty places in our
lives

Keeps on working to dispense
benefits even after the hug's
release

Besides, hugging prevents war.

# Qualifications

The qualifications for being a Hug Therapist and being a client are the same; just being.

Therapeutic hugging is a mutually healing process. In fact, hugger and hugged play interchangeable roles. As a Hug Therapist, you are open to the child within you who needs love, safety, support, caring, and play, and you are reaching

out to the same needs in
the other.

A Hug Therapist does not
blame or judge. But he or she
does recognise that many of
us, in our standoffish society,
have not learned to ask for the
emotional support we need. If
love or support — or play —
has been skimpy since
childhood, we may feel
wounded. If the twistings of
growing up have left us with
low self-esteem, we may feel

unlovable — unhuggable.

Hug Therapists can't solve all these problems, but they can respect the struggles and offer understanding, laughter, gentle words, and an abundance of hugs.

Hug Therapy is not just for the lonely or hurting ones. Hug Therapy can make the healthy healthier, the happy happier, and the most secure among us feel even more so.

Hugging is for everybody.

Anyone can be a Hug Therapist.  But if you master the Types of Hugs and the Advanced Techniques presented in this book, you will develop further skills and confidence in your natural ability to share wonderful hugs.

# Ethics and rules of conduct

When you are a truly professional Hug Therapist, you take full responsibility for what you say or do. Therefore the hugs you share must be thoughtful, respectful, and care-filled.

These are understood rules of conduct for Hug Therapists:

1. *Since Hug Therapy is always nonsexual, hug*

*accordingly*.  Be sure that the hugs you dispense are compassionate, not passionate.  A caring, comforting, or playful hug is different from a lover's embrace.  We usually recognise the difference.

No.

If you started out offering or wanting a supportive hug, and it has taken on overtones of greater physical intimacy, just recentre your feelings and thoughts on the original purpose of the hug — to give mutual support.

If you are clear about the kind of hug you are giving, the other hugger most likely will respond in kind. If not, you may want to have a talk about the importance of just-friendly hugs in your relationship.

Yes.

2. *Be certain you have permission before giving a hug.* Often permission to hug is implicit in a relationship. Your sweetheart or a close friend probably will welcome hugs almost any time. However, you still need to respect the other's need for privacy and space.

Sometimes you will receive nonverbal permission from someone who wants a hug, and you respond spontaneously. Or pave the way to hugging with a simple comment like, 'I would like to give you a hug.' Respect the other's verbal and nonverbal messages. Most of the time you will be aware of what is needed and acceptable.

If you misread someone who did not find a hug comfortable, don't be concerned. For some, hugging is very hard; sometimes a sturdy trust must be built before they feel safe enough to hug. Although we Hug Therapists believe the gift of touch to be extremely important, the gift of acceptance is just as important!

Ask first.

3. *Also be sure to ask permission when you need a hug.* Hug Therapists are not only dispensers of hugs but recipients too. Huggers must sometimes be huggees. Hugging-for-health is a practice of sharing, rather than of just giving or just taking.

When you feel the need for a hug, say: 'I would like a hug, if it's all right with you.' Or, 'I could really use a huge hug right now — would you oblige?'

Or, 'How about a hug before I go off to work?' (or to a meeting or a match or an interview or whatever). A post-hug 'thank you' or 'that felt good' is an important validation of the other's support.

May I have this hug?

*4. Be responsible for expressing what you need and the way you want it.* Blaming others because we're not getting what we need from them is a common mistake we make in our relationships. Some are naturally fine-tuned and intuitive about others' needs and comforts. But most of us — especially if we are busy worrying about our own insecurities — need direct, explicit communication.

If we want more hugs, fewer hugs, ten-second hugs, or two-minute-over-easy hugs — any kind of hug that may be different from what we're getting — we need to say so. Then we have to be willing to compromise as well as to realise that we won't

always get exactly what we
want when we want it.

For some, hugging is very hard.

# Contraindications

While Hug Therapists are convinced that hugging is for everyone, a few doubters have trouble accepting Hug Therapy. They believe, erroneously, that the sole purpose of a hug is to build a relationship of physical intimacy.

A physically intimate embrace can be beautiful too, but it meets a different level of

need. This kind of embrace
will never replace a good old
therapeutic hug! Even intimate
partners need bundles of
ordinary hugs too.

To keep little ones from
acquiring this narrow view of
hugs, hug them often —
affectionately, supportively,
playfully, and tenderly. Let
them see parents and other
adults hugging in these ways.
Otherwise they may grow up
believing that hugs are for

lovers only, and that in order to be hugged — and huggable — one must be physically attracted to the other hugger.

A Hug Therapist makes every effort to share the broader understanding of touch and hugging and the faith that a day filled with hugs can bring untold satisfaction and serenity.

# Fees

Hug Therapy is not free. The cost is the strength it requires to be vulnerable. The fee for hugging is the risk that our hugs will be rebuffed or misinterpreted.

When we are very young we are naturally open. We want to give love and touch as much as we want to get love and be touched. If we're deprived of

love and touch, we become
unwilling to pay the fee of
vulnerability. Love held back
can turn to pain.

Hug Therapists can help ease
this pain. When we risk our
hugs, we affirm our wonderful
ability to share. As we reach
out and touch others, we are
free to discover the
compassion — along with the
capacity for joy — that exists
in all of us. As we become
more spontaneous huggers and

find such inner riches, the fees
seem relatively small.

Thank goodness we have our
softer sides.

# Types of hugs

# Bear hug

In the traditional bear hug (named for members of the family Ursidae, who do it best), one hugger usually is taller and broader than the other, but this is not necessary to sustain the emotional quality of bear-hugging. The taller hugger may stand straight or slightly curved over the shorter one, arms wrapped firmly around the other's shoulders. The shorter of the pair stands straight with head against the taller hugger's shoulder or chest, arms wrapped — also firmly! — around whatever area between waist and chest that they will reach. Bodies are touching in a powerful, strong squeeze that can last five to ten seconds or more.

We suggest you use skill and forbearance in making the hug firm rather than breathless.

Always be considerate of your partner, no matter what style of hug you are sharing.

The feeling during a bear hug is warm, supportive, and secure.

Bear hugs are for:

Those who share a common feeling or a common cause.

Parents and offspring. Both need lots of reassuring bear hugs.

Grandparents and grand

off-spring. Don't leave
grandparents out of family
bear hugs.

Friends (this includes marrieds and lovers, who hopefully are friends too).

Anyone who wants to say, wordlessly, 'You're terrific!' Or, 'I'm your friend; you can count on me.' Or, 'I share whatever pain or joy you're feeling.'

*What can a bear hug say for you?*

# The A-frame hug

Stand facing each other,
wrapping arms around
shoulders, sides of heads
pressed together and bodies
leaning forward and not
touching at all below shoulder
level. There. You have an A-
frame hug. The length of time
spent in the A formation is
usually brief, since this is
often a 'hello' or 'goodbye'
hug.

The underlying feeling may be one of polite caring or detached warmth.

The A-frame hug is most appropriate for new acquaintances or professional colleagues, or in situations that require a degree of formality. Because it is relatively nonthreatening, it is comfortable for shy or unpractised huggers.

This is a classic hug and should not be discounted

because of its formal quality.
It has broad application and is
therefore beneficial to a wide
range of huggers.

An A-frame hug is particularly
apt for:

A great-aunt whom you haven't
seen since you were a toddler.

Your spouse's employer's
husband.

Your former academic adviser.

A new daughter-in-law.
*Who else?*

Like this.

# Cheek hug

The cheek hug is a very tender, gentle hug that often has a spiritual quality. It can be experienced comfortably sitting down, standing up, or even with one sitting and one standing, as full body contact is not necessary.

If you are both seated, turn comfortably towards each other and press the sides of your

faces together cheek
to cheek.  One hand may
be on the other's back and
the other supporting the back
of the head to counteract
the pressure of your cheek.
Breathe slowly and deeply.
Within a few seconds you will
feel very relaxed.  The cheek
hug often stirs deep feelings of
kindness, especially when
participants are close friends.

A cheek hug is a tasteful way to:

Greet an elderly friend or a relative who is seated.

Say a wordless 'I'm sorry' about a friend's disappointment.

Share a friend's joy at a happy occasion, like a wedding or graduation. (This is a considerate hug for congratulating the principals in reception lines, since it does

not tangle wedding veils or
crush boutonniéres.)

*At what times would you
proffer a cheek hug?*

It often has a spiritual quality.

# Sandwich hug

The sandwich hug is a lesser known variety, but once you experience its warmth and security, you'll want to share this one often.

This is a hug for three. Two face each other with the third in the middle facing either one of the others. Each of the two on the outside reaches towards the waist area of the other and hugs. The one in the centre wraps arms around the waist of the facing hugger. As an option, the outside pair may hug around the shoulders and all three snuggle heads together. The bodies are touching cosily.

The sandwich hug gives the one in the middle an especially secure feeling, which is helpful if she or he is going through a difficult time and needs extra support.

The sandwich hug is handy for:

Three good friends.

A couple wishing to comfort someone.

Two parents and a child. The child may be very young, grown up, or any place between.

*Make your own sandwich.*

# Grabber-squeezer hug

The grabber-squeezer hug
holds the record for brevity.
One hugger runs up to and
throws arms about another,
gives a fast squeeze before
letting go, then dashes off.
The one so hugged must be
alert in giving a squeeze in
return, in order to receive
maximum benefit from this hug.

In a variation of the grabber-squeezer, choreographically more difficult, both run towards each other and give a quick, simultaneous squeeze. Safety note: Avoid a collision course. The full-force crash of two bodies who have hurtled together or the knocking of two heads may negate some of the good feelings!

Feelings vary with the situation, but often the grabber-squeezer is accompanied by a sense of affectionate distraction because one or both of the huggers are rushed. If the huggee is not expecting it, there also may be a feeling of surprise.

Grab-and-squeeze hugging is a practical way to work in a lot of fast hugging when you're on a tight schedule. For more effective stress management, also include a liberal sprinkling of hugs that are gentler and last longer.

Use the grabber-squeezer:
In the workshop or the kitchen.
To wish someone luck before a
performance.

As a silent translation of the
words 'I like you a lot, but I'm
in a terrible hurry!'

*How can the grabber-squeezer
fit into your life?*

There also may be a feeling
of surprise.

# Group hug

The group hug is a very
popular hug for good friends
sharing in an activity or
project.  As Hug Therapists,
we would like the group hug to
be better known and more
often applied, just because it
feels so good.

The group forms a circle — its
members standing as close
together as possible, arms

around shoulders or waists —
and squeezes.  In a variation,
group hug participants, holding
each other as above, move in
towards the centre, shrinking
the circle.  They huddle
together for several moments,
then back up and break apart
with a cheer or sigh or a quick,
parting squeeze.

Besides good feelings of
support, security, and
affection, group hugs often
impart a sense of unity and

universal belonging.
Group hugs are good for:
Growth groups.
Support groups.
Classmates, teammates.
Hardworking committees.
Any bunch you like.
*When would your group
welcome a hug like this?*

A group hug often imparts a
sense of universal belonging.

# Side-to-side hug

The side-to-side hug, or the
lateral squeeze, is a great hug
to get and give while walking
along together. As you stroll
side by side with an arm
around the other's waist or
over the shoulder, once in a
while give a generous
squeeze.
This is also a merry and
playful hug for those moments

when you are standing in line with a friend.  It makes queuing up a pleasure!

The side-to-side hug provides a joyful moment while:

Walking to a bus.

On a hike or an archaeological dig.

Waiting to get into a Saturday night movie or to register for next term's classes.

When could you use a side-to-side hug?

# Back-to-front hug

In the back-to-front hug (also known as the waist-grabber), the hugger approaches the other from the back, folds arms around his or her waist and gives a gentle hug.

The back-to-front waist-grabber is the perfect hug to give someone who is peeling potatoes, scrubbing pans over a kitchen sink, or otherwise engaged in some routine stand-up chore. A somewhat old-fashioned hug, this was practised more extensively before the invention of the automatic dishwasher. But most of the time a waist-grabber is still welcome as a brief, playful gesture. The feeling behind it is happy and supportive.*

*Even more supportive would be the back-to-front hug followed by the picking up of a teatowel and applying it to the pans.

Back-to-front hugs are for:

Househusbands, housewives, and other live-ins.

Co-workers on an assembly line.

Friends whose occupations require that they face mostly in one direction — like raspberry-pickers or mail-sorters.

*Do you know someone who would appreciate a waist-grabber?*

# Custom-tailored hug

The most effective hug for you
is the hug that feels right,
considering the setting, the
situation, the one you are with,
and what you personally need
from the hug (affection,
strength and support,
reaffirmation of a bond of
friendship, relaxation, or any
other good feeling that a hug
can bring.)

Sometimes a custom-tailored hug is called for, as in the case of an extra-tall hugger and a very short huggee (or vice versa). Or when the hug, in order to please both parties equally, has to include a jealous pet or a favourite toy too.

Be creative. True Hug Therapists do not let circumstances stand in their way.

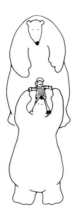

A custom-tailored hug may have
to include a favourite toy.

# Hugs: where, when, why

# Environments

A place of beauty enhances
the experience of hugging.
Whatever setting you consider
beautiful — a peaceful country
path on a warm, clear day or a
scrap of green park that opens
a city to the sky — can make
the hug you share with a friend
even more special.

However, if the setting seems
shabby or bleak, it can be

totally transformed just
because you are sharing a
hug.

Any place is the right place for
hugging when the heart is
open.

A hug transforms a bleak
setting . . .

. . . into a lovely place.

# Time of the day

Some are morning,
up-and-at-'em huggers.
Some are evening, thank-
heaven-the-day-is-over
huggers.  Some like to hug
at high noon on lunch
hours or at teatime.  Although
routine hugs are fine,
sometimes the most
appreciated hugs happen
spontaneously at unexpected
moments.

Friendship

Compassion

The feelings that bring on a hug — affection, sympathy, caring, just plain joy — can happen at any time of day. So can hug situations, like bumping into an old school friend at an airport. True Hug

Joy

Feelings that bring on a hug . . .

Therapists will entertain the idea of a hug at any time.  And hugs scattered through the day will help to maintain a sense of well-being, belonging, and self-esteem.

. . . can happen any time.

# Advanced techniques

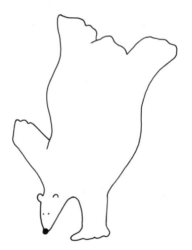

# Visualisation

Visualisation is a powerful
technique for learning and
change. One way we learn is
through repeated imprintings
on our minds — not only of
what we actually view in the
world around us, but also of
pictures we see in our
imaginations. Imagined
pictures, which can affect us
as strongly as reality,
sometimes even set off
physical responses.

Think about slicing a juicy lemon and squeezing the tart juice into your mouth. Your mouth waters at the very thought. You may detect a sour taste too. You have the sensation of sucking a lemon even though there's no real lemon anywhere in sight.

Now try visualising yourself hugging somebody. Let this imagined hug register in your mind as a nourishing experience. A mind picture like this can teach you to see yourself as someone who is at ease giving and getting warm, caring hugs.

In guided imagery, you plan or guide the direction you'd like your imagination to take. So let's say you would like to be comfortable greeting a friend with a heart-centred hug. Sit in a comfortable, quiet place and close your eyes. Breathe slowly and deeply four or five

An imagined hug is a nourishing
experience.

times and let your body relax totally. Imagine yourself walking along and meeting a good friend. Picture the two of you saying hello by putting your arms around each other and sharing a heart-centred hug.

Keep the picture in your mind as you sense good feelings of affection and warmth. It is important to put the imagined picture and the feelings together.

Or use guided imagery when you are feeling the need for support after a stressful day. Visualise a favourite friend who is also a good hugger giving you a very fond and supportive hug. Imagine that friend holding you and offering you reassurance and love. Keep the picture and the feelings in your mind for as long as you need comfort.

# Zen hugging

You can use any type of hug for Zen hugging. Our favourites are the cheek-to-cheek hug or the heart-centred hug. A very connected touch — a feet-to-feet and hands-to-hands touch, for instance — will do fine too.

Your eyes may be open or closed. Focus on your breathing, and allow it to become even and deep. You will begin to feel yourself relaxing. You are centred in the present moment. Let go of all thinking. All that is present is the experience of your senses.

You are aware of the warmth you are sharing, of your breath moving in and out, of the touch of the other person, of the air on your skin. Relax. Be suspended in time. The longer

you are able to relax in the
present moment, the deeper
will be your experience of the
hug or the touching.

Peace.

You are centred in the present
moment.

# Institute of hug therapy

We believe more must be done to break down the cultural and emotional barriers that prevent us from experiencing the healthy nourishment of touching and hugging. The establishment of the Institute of Hug Therapy is our whimsical, but earnest, contribution to that effort.

Becoming a member of the Institute of Hug Therapy is

easy. Just believe in the power of hugging! Wear the title of Hug Therapist proudly. Tell others about hugging for health. Spread the pro-hug philosophy wherever you go.

Hugging should not be something you do once in a while, at family reunions or birthdays or when one of your teammates makes a goal. Our hope is that hugging will become commonplace, without detracting from the

specialness of each separate
hug.

Hug often.  Hug well.

# THE SECOND
# TINY BOOK OF
# HUGS

. . . because we are all holding
each other through a dance of
joy and love.

# About speaking with hugs

Sorry

Thanks

Hello

Au Revoir

Peace

Whoopee

# Theory

Science and instinct tell us
that one good way to reach the
sensitive living spirit is
through physical touch. And
one of the most important
forms of touch is a hug. With
a hug, we communicate as
individuals on the deepest
level. With a hug, we embrace
the whole of life.

We all have an inner yearning
that calls us to respond with a

quality of contact that affirms
our potential as growing
individuals.  The language of
hugs nourishes the spirit.

We support
each other.

An embrace creates a circle of
compassion that promotes
growth and healing and feeds
our empty hearts.

# Application

Say it with hugs to emphasise the message.

We may say aloud, 'Let me know if there's any way I can help.' A hug adds, *I really mean that!*

We may say aloud, 'I like you.' A hug adds, *I care deeply about you. In fact, I love you a lot.*

Punctuate with a hug!

Say it with hugs when words are awkward or hard to say.

We may know the appropriate words but find them really difficult to say out loud, especially if we're shy or overwhelmed by feelings. At such times we count on the language of hugs.

A hug can say things like:

*I am here for you any time.*

*I really understand your feelings.*

*Please celebrate my joy with me.*

*Allow me to share in your sadness.*

Even ordinary words like hello and goodbye are sometimes very hard to say.

Please let me help you bear this
frightening time.

Say it with hugs when words
can't express it.

Although we may speak from
our most authentic selves as
we reach into our deepest
feelings, talk can only go so
far. An embrace from the
heart often cannot be
translated into words.

When we allow ourselves to be
in a still place of inner
awareness, the message of
vitality, spirit, and love that we
all carry within us is often felt,

given, and received in a place
beyond language.  To reduce
this experience to words,
either inwardly or out loud,
may diminish a very profound
message.

Besides using the magnificent
gift of language, we must
also respect intuitive,
wordless wisdom and listen
with our hearts.  That is how
we hear the greater meaning of
the mystery we have
named love.

Hugs have their own language.

# Ethics

A healing hug never gives a
mixed message. Instead, a
hug always speaks
authentically about who we are
and what we feel; we need first
to be in touch with ourselves
before we can reach out to
touch someone else. We are
uncomfortable and confused
when words say one thing and
an embrace says another.

I feel just wonderful. Everything
is A-okay.

I'm really very sad.

A hug never says *I blame you*
*or I want to cause harm.*

We are all complex individuals
trying to find fulfilment. We
do not have a choice about
how we feel, but we can
choose what we say or do in
response to feelings.

We can discover ways to meet
our needs without blaming or
harming ourselves or others.
As Hug Therapists, our
responsibility is to create and
heal, not to harm or blame.

We can no longer afford to view the world in terms of 'good guys' and 'bad guys'.

A therapeutic hug is always nonsexual.

A caring, supportive, or playful hug is different from a lover's embrace and does not invite the level of physical intimacy that is part of a romantic relationship.

I want to be your lover, baby.
No.

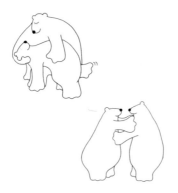

I want to be your friend.  Yes.

# Basics of hug language

Besides its particular message, a hug to be truly therapeutic always makes these nonverbal statements.

A therapeutic hug always says:

*I understand how you feel.*

Because we feel the same kinds of feelings, there is a bond of commonality that embraces us and creates unity. We respect our own feelings as a natural guidance system for making decisions, creating values, and working through problems.  We validate each other's feelings as an essential part of being.

Your loss is my loss
That's too bad.

A therapeutic hug always says:

*I respect your unique inner
wisdom.  You are special.*

We celebrate the fact that
within the circle of unity are
individuals whose rich
diversity makes life exciting.
Others' feelings, ideas, and
values expand our reality
beyond our limited and
personal views.  The world is
full of endless possibilities
because we are different.

A therapeutic hug always says:

*You are who you are, not just what you do.*

We all need the confirmation of ourselves as whole and unique beings separate from the many functional roles we must play.

Example: *You are not only a doctor and a mother as well as a pitcher in a softball league and a veterinary assistant and an aerobics expert and an arbiter of disputes and a lover and a bus driver and a*

*domestic genius — you are*
*YOU.*

Have a hug, Clement.

A review of the most often used hugs is helpful in order to choose just the right hug to convey the message. Each hug which follows has many verbal and nonverbal translations depending on the huggers and the situation; just a few are offered here.

# A dictionary of hugs

# Ankle hug

Firm encirclement of another's
ankle, usually by a hugger of
small stature. Requires an
immediate response, such as
being picked up and given a
bear hug. Differs from an
ordinary tackle because of the
hugger's feelings of love and
need — and the huggee's
feeling of warmth at being
needed.

The ankle hug invariably says:
*I am smaller than you are now,*

*and I count on you.*
*Just touching you gives me*
*security.*

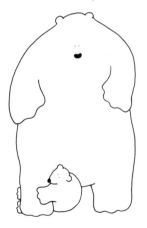

# 'Guess who?' hug

A frolicsome hug for longtime friends. Makes a gentle game out of an ordinary 'hello' or 'good day' greeting.

A 'guess who' hug has this to say:

*If you guess who I am, I'll be happy you've thought about me. If you don't — well, mystery is part of the fun too.*

We mustn't overlook the fact
that humour is absolutely
necessary for our well-being.

# Heart-centred hug

Undistracted and unhurried.
Perhaps the highest form of
hugging.  Acknowledges that
place at the centre of each of
us where pure, unconditional
love may be found.

*A heart-centred hug says:*

*Feel our oneness as our bond
of friendship grows.*

*I may frown on your
naughtiness or misbehaviour,*

*but I don't love you any less.*

Let's forgive each other —
grudges are uncomfortable.

# Sandwich hug

A three-way hug. Especially secure for the one in the middle.

Some messages of a sandwich hug:

*Let's affirm our deep feeling of family closeness.*

*We're all equal shareholders in this friendship.*

*Let's make sure none of us is ever left out.*

# Side-to-side hug

Also known as a lateral squeeze. A merry, playful aside. Use it while strolling together or waiting in line.

Listen to what a side-to-side hug has to say:

*Waiting around for gates to open is not a bit tedious because you're with me.*

*Being with you makes me feel good — wherever we are.*

# Top-of-the-head hug

Or cranial clasp.

Firm, supportive, strength-giving. Usually offered to a seated huggee by a standing hugger. A gift of power to one who is feeling stunned or frail or depressed.

The cranial clasp gives a clear message of strength:

*Tap into my positive energy if you are feeling helpless today.*

*I'm ready to share my strength
with you for as long as you
need it.*

# Variations

Of course each basic hug type
has numerous variations.  If
you are well-versed in these
types and what each can say,
you can augment your hug-
message vocabulary
limitlessly.

I'm here, Melissa.

Let's do hugs.

Scuba dooby doo.

You're really handy, Harriet.

Pas de deux

# Say it with hugs

As your hugging vocabulary
grows, you will find that the
wonderful language of hugs is
perfectly adapted to conveying
everyday messages, especially
in the areas of communication
which follow.

# Safety
# Security
# Trust

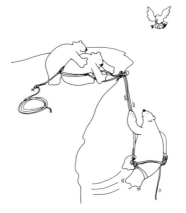

## A HUG SAYS SAFETY

Regardless of our age or status in life, we all need to feel safe. When we do not feel safe, our actions may become inefficient, our interactions with others may lose their pleasure.

A hug creates a warm circle of support so that we can return to our tasks with a renewed sense of safety.

A hug says, *In my arms is a*

*place where you can feel safe.*

A hug-for-safety statement is needed:

when stepping up to a podium to give a talk a hug says, *No need for accordion knees — just imagine everyone in the audience giving you a safe hug.*

when graduating — from anywhere a hug says, *You will find safe places in your new life too.*

when the night is full of
shifting shadows a hug says,
*Daylight will show you that
shadows are really the safe
shapes of ordinary things.*

Try a heart-centred hug to shut
out fears and pass along a
message of safeness.

You are safe here.  Morning will
come soon.

A hug keeps back the shadows.

## A HUG SAYS SECURITY

Everyone needs to feel secure, but especially those on both ends of the age spectrum who depend on the love and good will of those who care for them.

A hug-for-security statement is needed:

by the very youngest trying out steps for the first time a hug says, *When the world you set out to explore seems frightening and complex, you*

*can return any time to the*
*security of my arms until you*
*are ready to go out again and*
*discover more.*

by the oldest trying out steps for the first time after recovering from a fall a hug says, *I will not allow you to become your infirmity or lose your specialness or dignity or your importance to me.*

Try a side-to-side or cheek hug to say security.

## A HUG SAYS TRUST

Trust comes from the sense of
security and safety we receive
from others. Trust can free us
to move when fear overwhelms
our desire to participate in the
exciting challenges of life.

Give a learn-to-trust hug
message to:

a youth who needs
reassurance that he is not
alone in the difficult task of
facing new responsibilities

a hug says, *You do not have to do more or go faster or higher until you are ready. You can trust me to be here and support you through your journey into the adult world.*

a friend beginning a new venture in a new location with new associates a hug says, *Please take with you the feelings of trust you have learned here. I will continue to be your friend wherever you are.*

Sometimes a quick side-to-side
hug is enough to reinforce a
message of trust.

If you start to tip over, I'll be
here.

You can
trust us.

I trust you.

# Self-worth
# Belonging

## A HUG SAYS SELF-WORTH

Self-worth is the foundation for satisfaction and success in our lives. This sense of personal value is created from the moment of birth, mostly by the messages others give us about ourselves.

Because the validation passed from generation to generation is often incomplete, many of us did not learn about our full worth when we were young. Now we have the

chance to continue the
process of affirmation, by
giving the message through
our hugs that we recognise
the excellence of each
individual.

A hug proclaims the innate
worth of anyone:

a runner who does not quite
qualify for a marathon, an
actress who muffs her lines, a
chef whose souffle flattens, a
batter who swings hard, but
strikes out

a hug says, *Self-worth and success are not synonyms. Trying is valuable. Being is valuable. Above all, YOU are valuable.*

one who has grown up with an uncomfortable sense of inadequacy, or even shame a hug says, *I have a real respect and affection for you. Please let me help you change your negative perceptions about yourself.*

Try a bear hug to pass along self-worth. (If the one you wish to hug is shy or fears intimacy, a gentler hug — like a cheek hug or a cranial clasp — may be more appropriate.)

You are wonderful, worthy, noble, kind, and interesting.

Also huggable.

## A HUG SAYS BELONGING

Our sense of worth expands when we feel we belong — first to intimate groups of relatives and friends, then to the amazing family of living creatures everywhere.

When we feel our place within the embrace of this universal connection, our hugs invite others into the circle of life.

When 'I' becomes 'we', a hug speaks ardently of the warmth of belonging:

for anyone who is part of a
group sharing an ideal, a
project, a common interest,
a game, a trade or
profession or who is lucky
enough just to have a
bunch of good friends a hug
says, *Your separateness and
my separateness add
something unique and
wonderful to this team we're
part of.*

*This fellowship gives my life
meaning.*

A group hug can be the greatest voice of all for self-worth and belonging.

# Strength
# Healing

## A HUG SAYS STRENGTH

We often think of strength as a solitary energy that develops out of an individual's determination and toughness and self-responsibility. Of course responsibility-for-self is essential for personal power. But we can still pass along our inner vitality as a gift to others — to confirm and sustain their own strength and power.

Strength, particularly, is communicated as a bodily

message. Touching and
hugging are energising. The
wonder is: when we seek to
transfer our energy in a hug,
our own strength increases!

Sometimes you lean on me.

Give a gift-of-strength hug:

to someone left alone when a relationship dissolves a hug says, *When your faith in others has been damaged, let me hold you and fill you with strength.*

to a child feeling confused after a parent has moved away from home a hug says, *You are not responsible for your parents' happiness. You have good friends in the world outside — and I'm one of them.*

to a not-so-young athlete,

retiring from the game a hug says, *There are other strengths besides physical prowess. I honour what you have achieved. But most of all I really like who you are and who you will be.*

A heart-centred or bear hug is a strength-giving statement.

Sometimes I lean on you.

## A HUG SAYS HEALING

Our strength becomes a
powerful healing force when
given through physical contact.
We have heard many-times-
told stories of healing through
touch.  Now scientific research
continues to confirm that
touching and holding impart a
life energy that heals — as
well as supports and comforts
— those suffering from illness
or disease.  New studies show
that, to be truly therapeutic,

touching must be coupled with an intent to help and to heal. Casual, offhand touching is less effective.

The vitality we receive from a therapeutic embrace contains this healing message: *I am alive and whole and I am coming home to my self.*

Give a healing hug to:

anyone who is trying to shake off an illness or infection or a bout with the blues, or whose

broken body or spirit is
mending a hug says, *I will hold
you so that you can draw
strength from my support while
you heal.*

*My strength combined with
yours is more than the sum of
both our strengths. Feel that
remarkable energy flowing into
making you whole again!*

A top-of-the-head hug speaks
respectfully about healing.

Though I have confidence in my own skill, I also respect the miracle of your self-healing. I recognise a healing force that is more powerful than either of us.

Rx:

Four hugs a day for survival

Eight hugs a day for
maintenance

Twelve hugs a day for growth

# Appreciation
# Happiness
# Celebration

## A HUG SAYS APPRECIATION

Appreciation for others and gratitude for the abundance and variety of life — these are flavours of happiness we communicate in an embrace.

When we are filled with thankfulness and appreciation, our hugs proclaim, *I'm grateful today for the deliciousness of life. Let's be sure to take the time to taste the richness of each moment.*

Let a hug voice your appreciation for:

a favourite teacher a hug says, *Thank you for making learning a never-ending adventure for me.*

a benefactor or a sponsor a hug says, *I am grateful for the miracles you help bring about in my life.*

one who offers you a new contract or career a hug says, *Thanks for the fresh challenge*

— and for your faith in me.

a parent (now that you're grown up) a hug says, *What a great experience to know you now as an adult friend!*

someone whose words have inspired you a hug says, *Your messages have brought me serenity and helped me grow spiritually.*

a comic or jester a hug says, *Thanks for your cleverness and creative clowning.*

*You make us whole*
*as you make us laugh.* An
appreciative hug can be any
kind — from a side-to-side to a
waist-grabber — depending on
the degree of closeness you
feel towards the huggee.

I appreciate your humour.
Hug a clown.

## A HUG SAYS HAPPINESS

Wonder, excitement, humour, contentment, and serenity are some of the shades of happiness that colour our lives. When we live under a rainbow of these good feelings, our hearts overflow with an abundance of joy — so much joy that we have trouble NOT sharing it!

It's a delight to communicate our pleasure with a hug that says, *What a great day! I'm feeling so alive and wonderful! I'm overjoyed to share the excitement of this moment with you!*

Pass on the exhilarating lyrics of a happiness hug to:

your cohort in the discovery of a new idea a hug says, *What's more exciting than exchanging thoughts and finding an entirely new concept that makes life's pieces fit together!*

your golf or tennis partner a
hug says, *It's really a kick —
just to be here with you,
moving freely and laughing
over the crazy things that
happen in a game.*

a new friend beside you in a
beautiful place — a lakeside, a
hilltop, a street at festival time
a hug says, *Wow! What a
view! What a place! I'm
excited that you can see it with
me.*

A quick back-to-front hug or grabber-squeezer heralds your happiness.

## A HUG SAYS CELEBRATION

Celebration often means joining with others to share in the delight of a memorable event. We applaud and sing and feast and dance and laugh and cry at rituals that give meaning to our lives.

On these occasions we really need the language of hugs. A warm embrace is the happiest reward for a special moment, and says, *I am honoured to be with you and to take part in these festivities.*

A back-to-front hug or bear hug, sandwich or group hug, custom-tailored or side-to-side hug — in fact, any kind of hug at all — sings out, *Let's celebrate!*

Yes!

But we don't have to wait for a special occasion to celebrate. We can celebrate who we are any time — here, now, sharing this world of marvels and miracles with those we care about.

We celebrate, too, our wonderful ability to communicate with hugs.

The language of hugs helps us speak from our hearts.

The language of hugs helps us see our true selves.

You are not really a bear.

You are not a bear either.

# That extra touch

All of us need not only hugs,
but other kinds of respectful
touching as well. For some,
hugging may even be
uncomfortable. It may cause
feelings of distress or fear
because of cultural
conditioning, physical trauma,
or emotional deprivation.
Sometimes just gently holding
a hand, or giving a validating

pat on the back, a playful head rub, a relaxing neck massage, or a kind touch on the arm may be a more sensitive way to communicate support.

Remember, although touching and hugging are of extraordinary value, the most cherished gift we can give is our acceptance of others' unique feelings and needs. This means that our decision to communicate through hugs or touch must always be based

on respect for what is
comfortable for that person.

Hug well. Hug often